C. M. HERZOG

ONCE THERE WAS EDEN

GLOOMY SONNETS AND OTHER POEMS

Bibliografische Information der Deutschen Bibliothek
Die Deutsche Bibliothek verzeichnet diese Publikation
in der Deutschen Nationalbibliografie;
detaillierte bibliografische Daten sind im Internet über
http://dnb.dnb.de abrufbar.

1. Auflage
1st edition

© C. M. Herzog, Mag. Artium
Herstellung und Verlag:
BoD – Books on Demand, Norderstedt, 2020
ISBN: 9 783752 673173

Printed in Germany

INDEX

THE PLAGUE

Our country is bewitch'd with an evil plague!

Bubonic plague, we shun thee more than ever!

No more a priest shall teach, a whore shall brag!

Survival in the first place we endeavor!

Foul-smelling bulges before the gates of hell,

where our old foes in fiery rainfall must dwell.

Where is the court, where any plaintiff speaks?

No man is still prepared to file a claim!

The boat is on the ocean, yet it leaks,

no one is leaving, no one's there to blame!

Around the banks of the Thames some rats are running

into the city, where few cats are cunning.

And what about that wig? There is a flea jump!

The little beasts contaminate your hair!

And in your face there is a swelling flea bump,

whence blood is dribbling quickly, do you care?

- Oh yes, this is a wicked thing indeed!

- So cut the bulge and simply make it bleed.

The street is full of bodies of the dead,

who're left out there and give an evil smell.

No passer-by will stop and bow his head

in this demonic scene, none rings the bell.

No more shall law and order rule this empire

and no one face the judge to raise the sham higher.

In all this kingdom pestilence fiercely rules

and takes away the hopes of its bravest knight.

Some doctors are as stubborn as their mules,

refuse their help to end this filthy plight.

Hard liquor is the medicine of the hour

and men are drunk and get their foolish power.

Some doctors wear the masks of birds of prey

and treat their patients in vain by venesection.

This is the first step reaching for decay.

Not even dying men will receive affection.

Whoever can, will leave infested ground

and burn the bridges, blow the trumpet sound.

ROMAN SACRIFICE

Verbena bundles spread their fragrant smell

upon an altar, made of marble stone.

The priests who in Jove's holy temples dwell

burned all the incense and a lion's bone.

They chanted sadly, melodies from heaven,

with trembling voices, altogether seven.

A bull was drawn into the holy temple

next to the altar, fearfully he cried,

and with his feet the bull began to trample

on holy ground; his fate he so defied.

The high priest then commenced the sacrifice

of this poor animal, who knew no vice.

His blood was caught in a receptacle,

and each observer, piously, knelt down;

this was a venerated spectacle

which taught the audience to win the crown:

Hoping for life, the faithful crowd should learn

to die themselves, serenity to earn.

The bull fell down, abandoning his spirit,

believers, grieving, lifted up their hands.

The roughest natures, shunning death, still fear it,

just like the bull's life, all things come to ends.

They prayed to Jove, the highest-ranking God:

"Show us thy grace, oh Jove, mislead us not!"

RIDDLES

I spoke to you in riddles and disguise,

but the ambiguous words have long been clear:

The past induced myself to tell you lies,

what you hear now, is just the truth, my dear!

I searched for you in vain, but still I know

that you are there and know each single word.

And in the end when you will truly show,

each single word, I guess, will then be heard.

There is a reason that I want you near:

You give me comfort and a place in life.

I've seemed to understand, since you've been here,

my reasons and the best for which I strive.

So what you get is not of money's worth,

and what I get, is good to end my dearth.

KABBALAH

The lord of darkness fading in the shadow,

the lord of heaven fading in the sky;

some tender sunrays falling on the meadow,

and in the sky some tiny clouds pass by.

Your proper name divides into its letters,

and you compose them to the name again.

And while the peaceful world around you shatters,

you come to senses, and at last you're sane.

There is some danger in the book of verses,

but when you get it, you can get it right.

And in the end you overcome the curses

that have no purpose in the sweet sunlight.

The secret is to let your thoughts drift by

and cling to nothing, let your senses fly.

KING OF HEARTS

In autumn, when the brownish leaves fall down,

you see the mighty king of hearts appear.

You follow him, without a doubting frown,

he drives away all bitterness and fear.

His voice is sweeter than the lovely song

of rose-winged angels in the starry sky.

And in his presence you will do no wrong,

whilst in his hands the world's best secrets lie.

Reach out for him, and he may disappear;

without him, life is cold and dark and blue.

Yet if you know that he is always near,

his tender presence makes your dreams come true.

ACE OF HEARTS

You opened up the game and shook the cards,

I took my share and played the ace of hearts;

you were so cruel, nailed me to the cross,

my ace of hearts is bleeding, what a loss!

Don't play this evil game until the end,

I didn't mean to play against a friend.

My heart is bleeding, and I feel the pain,

I gave myself to slaughter and was slain.

Why do you hurt a soul that needs you true?

An enemy would do the things you do!

WORDS TO A FRIEND

I plead not that the words I said are wrong,

although I know that you will never see

what I have tried to tell you for so long,

that is, you are a precious friend to me.

Yet friends will hardly act the way you do,

they give me shelter, when the tide comes in.

But still I mean to be a friend to you,

for it was you, who made my life begin.

This is the life I've lead for years on end,

where my success is easily obtained.

Where is the helpful hand you proved to lend,

when this performance is, indeed, sustained?

Push me away, and wait if I come back!

Your pity is no honor that I lack!

FREEDOM

A life deprived of meaning is not worth

the effort that it takes to make things go,

and in this everlasting state of dearth

no man would strive to let his feelings show.

It is the state, where life itself is pain

or just a game, in which you play some role.

And it would take an effort to stay sane,

but nothing really matters on the whole.

If anything, at least you live in peace,

for life might certainly be even worse.

But then, you never really feel at ease,

the rotten game itself becomes a curse.

If anything, your life just slips away,

which doesn't matter, for you cannot stay.

Maybe there's a creator in the sky

who watches us and gives us our share,

for no illusion would be worth the try,

but this may be the reason, why we care.

With money you can't buy the shining stars,

and still they shine, and make your fears subside.

With money, you can buy some golden cars,

but in the end, the best things are denied.

When there is nothing you can lose, you're free,

but freedom is no state that I desire.

It happens, this is not the choice for me

and definitely nothing I admire.

So God is always watching from above

and all, that ever counts, is peace and love.

TIMES OF DARKNESS

In times of darkness, we retrieve

the values that are true.

Despite of fortune, we receive

the fruit of what we do!

Some men are kings, and they are crowned

and there is much to see,

so shall the noble be renowned

and live in luxury.

A poor man lies down on the ground

and waits for time to come,

and still his ways are fairly sound,

although he may be dumb.

He may achieve in his long life

the things he really needs,

whereas the noble man must strive

to plant the finest seeds.

Where is the soldier's friend at last?

He's drowned in tears and blood!

His enemy, who shot too fast,

is lying in the mud.

A slave comes right before the king

in all his royal pride.

"Your palace is no holy thing,

my honor is denied!

I'll show you what a black man can,

I'll surely get it right.

And then I will not face a ban:

I'm ready for the fight!

When there are things which he don't know,

a teacher's at a loss.

And then he tries hard not to show

that he is not the boss.

In every man there is some doubt

about the use of life.

And many actions are allowed,

the only must: to strive!

In times of darkness we retrieve

the values that are true.

Despite of failure, we receive

the fruit of what we do!

THE SCARLET THREAD

The cool face of the North wind blows

onto a dark red-colored rose,

and in a garden on a thread,

there is a pretty dark-brown cat.

He's sitting on a scarlet thread

next to the fragrant flower-bed.

So now we see the scarlet thread,

which reaches from the little cat

up to the North wind and the rose,

which shivers, as the cold wind blows.

You hear some laughter in the sky

with long-wing'd eagles flying high.

The sun is warm, the wind has blown.

This cat is sitting all alone

next to a rose, whose color's red;

in fact, the little cat is sad.

Though in his mouth, he's always had

the witty, far-stretched scarlet thread!

RAMSES

Dark-haired young Ramses smiling with delight:

The bull is scorning, and he roars with rage.

The native boy and this wild beast will fight,

the bull comes running from his wooden cage.

The boy shall win, the empire is his wage.

The sun god on the ocean shall stand still,

when Ramses runs ahead, prepared to kill.

The fight is over, and young women cry

with joy and love for this enormous king,

the wounded bull is on his way to die,

when Ramses leaves the bull, the stage, the ring.

"A fight like this can't mean so great a thing!"

The sun god on the ocean moves ahead,

the Pharaoh is praised, the bull is dead.

The sun god chose this young man for his pride,

his courage and his will to rule this land.

The gods of darkness scorned him, and they lied,

yet Ramses played his role until the end.

Old Egypt shall bow down, but Ramses stand!

The sovereign makes a vow before the sun:

Peace shall be kept, until my days are done!

In his own ranks he has some cruel foes,

who hate him and decide to kill him soon.

But as the fate of mighty Ramses goes,

he stays aware at night and high at noon.

And in the night, he's guided by the moon.

When once his enemies are there to fight,

he takes their lives, escapes this evil plight.

The pyramid, which hides his corpse today,

beneath the stars shall still reflect this wonder:

King Ramses died, his people went astray,

his soul shall stay alive, the world down-under,

when Egypt's splendor has finally fallen asunder.

The corpse of this young king is in decay,

and golden times of Egypt passed away.

MASONRY

You are a man of fifty years,

no wiser than a child.

Just fifty years of love and tears,

and you are also wild.

For man has lived a million years,

his ego must surrender.

He must defeat his inner fears,

so he becomes more tender.

I am as old as mankind now,

you are as old as I,

you understand the world somehow,

your mind, your soul can fly.

And you read Hamlet in your youth,

you know how he was slain.

You watch his conscience and the truth

within a play again.

You watch the conscience of the king,

you watch it as I do.

A fair play is the hardest thing,

this acting is untrue.

You say: To be or not to be?

This question I do fear:

So is it death or fantasy,

the answer is not clear.

It seems to be free masonry

and then again like hell.

When will you set the mason free

and ring the final bell?

When will the final curtain fall

and is the answer life?

You know that you hurt them all

and force them to survive.

Our mind is old a million years,

a million years past now.

What is not conscious, spreads the fears

we must defeat somehow.

And you can dive deep in your mind,

when there's no place to hide.

You need the shelter you can find

to scare the beasts aside.

KNOSSOS

On Crete, there is a treasure to discover,

which rises gently on a small green hill.

The ruins of Knossos by day uncover,

remainders of King Minos' palace still.

For time itself becomes a great illusion,

five-thousand years, you touch them with your hand.

And in this overwhelming great confusion

you get impressions of a foreign land.

The palace of the king will stand forever,

although the king himself is gone for good.

The mighty place is silent, and you never

can reach as much perfection as they could.

So Minos is now sitting on the throne,

eternity is clearly carved in stone.

CLAY

Like shadows in the darkness of the night

a man appears and disappears again.

It seems too hard to get the riddle right,

you get no honor, but receive disdain,

and still seek shelter, when you know you're slain.

Who is the king, and who the kingly guard?

The play is on, but winning it is hard!

And as in chess the figures move around

to win the kingdom of another land,

you start confusing images and sound,

the artist's word, a weapon in your hand.

The word will be the winner in the end.

Man's gift is to create the art of speech

and to pursue the aim he wants to reach.

A young man's view may differ from the age,

however, it exists in its own right.

A lion is imprisoned in a cage,

he needs to run about and see the light.

Yet lions are devoured by the night.

And maybe in the end there is a chance:

The feelings are like clay in our hands.

28

PROMETHEUS

The fallen angel seeks no more the lord,

in all his pride, he hides and looks away.

He gets no worship and no just reward,

whilst in his shadow all the angels stay.

This angel by himself created man

and gave him reason for the deep dark nights,

now he must shun the light in such a den

that bans the sun and all the sweet star lights.

The fallen angel lying at your feet

has realized that you are just a man.

And though you look like him and surely sweet

you cannot do what this dark angel can.

You act like god, but angels never cry,

you reign in hell, but angels never die.

FELONY

The princess wears a necklace and a ring,

the room is dark, her eyes reflect the light;

she's waiting for her father and the king

to share his secrets and his kingly pride;

which means the daughter's heart is open wide.

The father penetrates the daughter's room:

This is the day of incest and of doom.

The father, yearning for his daughter's breast,

gives in to sexual lust and to desire,

he feels his heart beat in his mighty chest

and is consumed by an orgasmic fire.

He says, he loves her, but he is a liar.

His daughter is no virgin any more,

and blood and sweat are trickling on the floor.

She weeps and trembles in her father's arm

(the daughter's eyes are dark as ebony),

though it appeared that he would do no harm:

The king himself commits this felony.

And in his mind he hears a symphony.

A blood stain spreading on the daughter's bed,

the fingers of the king are bloody red.

The palace is a witness to this crime,

but every mouth is shut and speaks no word.

The father goes unpunished in his time,

the daughter tries to speak and won't be heard.

The silent crime in memory is stirred.

And so the daughter's lips will speak no more,

but there remains a blood stain on the floor.

KINGDOM OF FRANCE

The palace yearns for lust and for desire

and full of joy, they crown the heir king.

To his sweet face the ancient gods aspire,

the sweetest choirs of the angels sing;

his sister offers him a golden ring.

The kingdom lying at his noble feet,

he watches all his army and his fleet.

His people shout and pray and wish him well:

The king is dead! Long live the king of France!

And brave young knights shall greet him with a bell.

The new crowned king just throws a hidden glance

at all the girls, who follow him and dance.

His beauty needs a mirror in each room,

and in his gardens thousand blossoms bloom.

A war in Holland is a fancy thing,

this heir lives for music and for ryhme.

And all his subjects worship him and sing,

they yearn for gold and pass a happy time.

And at their dinners, they have pantomime.

The arts shall blossom, and the arts shall rule,

concerning duties many hearts stay cool.

The old king was a man of grace and honor,

he spent his time with work and ruled in peace.

The old king was a very gentle donor:

He ruled by wisdom, and he felt at ease.

He was a guardian of the golden fleece.

The old king was a god in his own rows,

he seemed to be there when the sunshine rose.

The king is dead! Long live the king of France!

Some childish boy, a shame before the crown,

he spends his time with women and with dance

and tears the mighty kingdom slowly down.

The old men shake their heads, his servants frown.

He gives no hand, when people are in need,

is just a man of leisure and of greed.

There are some uproars in his father's land,

he is so scared and shuns the light of day

and wakes at night, until his mother's end,

his wife and children even run away.

The treasure of the palace turns to clay.

They have no bread, and thus his people die.

And in the night, he hears his father cry.

THE SNAKE

A tiger from the jungle roams the land,

a wicked snake, uncoiled, it creeps in the sand.

Its master is blowing the magic holy tune,

the poisonous snake is dancing under the moon.

His cobra's poison, dripping down on the ground,

the tiger roars, he's softly running around;

protecting the snake, the master's at a loss:

The cobra is servant to him, who is the boss.

Old India is shining with thousands of flickering lights,

the people shouting loud: The tiger fights!

The black snake moves, and poison may surely trickle

from its sharp teeth, its head is up and fickle.

The moonlight fades, giving in to the warmest sun,

and in the morning, the Egyptians stun:

The wild beasts keep on moving, eye in eye,

the snaking prey haunts the tiger passing by.

The master is crying over his dancing snake,

which is not yet defeated, and wide awake.

It bites the tiger in the heat of the sun,

the wounded tiger falls down, and tries to run.

And so the snake has ended this man-eater's life

and all the village people shall finally survive.

The charmer takes his snake up, and he blows

his well-known song, which rises from his toes.

RUINS OF TROY

The summer sun will rise above old Troy,

whilst stones of its old palace reassemble,

up on the mountain climbs a little boy,

Greek warriors shout out, their foes shall tremble,

the Trojan men shall die, they fall and shamble.

The summer sun makes Helen reappear,

the wedding's over, what remains is fear.

And poor Ulysses standing on a boulder

is witness to destruction and to murder,

a boy, who's sitting on a Greek man's shoulder,

he's crying, but the man will go no further.

He stops on a cliff, and he is not a birder.

The weapons of the Greek reflect the light

and leave the weeping ruins to the night.

Their courage, fading on their way to Greece,

the sea is full of danger and of riddle,

but anyway, they have the golden fleece,

the beast of darkness rises in the middle:

Skylla is great, the wooden ships are little.

The angry gods of Troy are wild and frowning,

and now the Greek invader's slowly drowning.

PHARAOH

Invisible heart of the sun,

which shines when the day work is done,

which guides you in spirit so right

through darkness in greatest delight.

Oh, Pharaoh, son of the light,

you've never shunned any fight,

you sit in the gold-woven sky

above all the clouds up high.

The milky way lies at your feet,

in darkness you shall meet

the everlasting sun,

before the night is done.

And lions sit still, when they say

that man is the catcher of prey;

yet lions roar loud when they hear,

their path is unhindered and clear.

They follow the fleeing game,

but even the lions grow tame

before the sun of the light,

who's eager to win and to fight.

He reigns by order and law,

they touch him with a paw,

he grabs it and sits still,

and so the lions will.

The fate of the Earth is the sun,

the sea is its spouse on the run,

the waters flow with noise

and all the fish rejoice.

Some diamonds are falling like rain

and touching the ground again,

the snow falls and covers them all,

and still, the season is fall.

Life is a fight and a test,

you got to reach out for the rest.

Enjoy it as much as you can:

The sun is the servant of man!

SHOAH

When Montezuma laid his feather crown

down on the floor before the Spanish priest,

the Spanish burnt his native people down,

until the reign of Montezuma ceased

to show its Indian pride, and to exist.

The natives saw the world from underneath,

and Spain received the golden flower wreath.

The Indians once reigned in paradise

right from the Ocean to the other coast,

they were like any sparrow, which gently flies

above the waters, and adored his ghost.

The white men came to conquer and to boast.

And Manitou, the god of earlier times,

was soon replaced by churches with their chimes.

When black men first were conquered by the white,

they bowed to earth, and served them with their lives,

the black men, who were strong, had not the might

to keep the white from taking all their wives.

The white men reigned, but soon they drew their knives.

The blacks were stolen like a piece of wood,

the filthy priests were covered with a hood.

The Jews just followed in this bloody row,

when Nazis took their honor and their life;

they feared, the awful crime would never show,

and no-one could believe their desperate strife.

And those, who did, had children and a wife.

The Nazi was a hero in his time

and gave the century a bloody crime.

Yes, Palestinians had their proper state

and raised their children under Muslim law;

the Jews encountered competitive hate,

and so this country's in the Western claw,

which kills the natives with its deadly paw.

The Muslims lost their state and civil rights

and often die in bombings and in fights.

THE COMET

The comet on its way to hit the Earth

is wandering throughout the starry night;

and if it comes, with it will come the dearth,

the cold, and an enormous, endless fight;

the sun which nowadays still shines so bright,

will stop its course, and throw us into hell,

where nothing grows and only ghosts shall dwell.

The space is wide, the Earth is not forlorn

yet spins in space in some odd galaxy,

but when entire continents are torn,

the spectacle we see in fantasy

reveals the planet's greatest mystery:

And if the endless ocean is the goal,

for mankind, too, the deadly bell will toll.

There is a chance that we won't live this day,

and that the planet will evade the crash,

this comet is still light-years far away,

a brand-new weapon, and it's caught in a mesh.

This makes the giant stone eventually dash.

We might invent a weapon to stay safe,

or it may be the Earth becomes a grave.

In all directions matter will expand,

each single planet has its proper tone,

to stay in orbit is the great demand,

the mystery of space is still unknown.

The creatures are, however, not alone.

Man will survive, he will not be forlorn,

because it was God's will that he was born.

SUNSET

A fisherman watches the deep blue sea,

entangled by all its mystery.

The deep sea rises with thunder

and thunderbolts flashing yonder.

The waives go up, and thunders crash,

and make the peaceful waters splash,

the storm turns slow and calm

and nature does no harm.

He's long been buried, but in a dash

young Phoenix is rising from the ash,

he spreads his wings and flies

into the cloudy skies.

Some dolphin cubs play full of joy,

they're jolly, but a little coy,

the fisherman by the shore

will watch their game no more.

The sun goes down, the boats are back,

upon his common beaten track

the fisherman goes home:

My cabin is my dome!

The sun gets in his ocean boat

and sets the sails, and sets afloat,

and high in the sky the moonlight

shines bright, and then it's soon night!

DRAGONS AND LIONS

Behold your king! He is the foremost man

in all his country! All the fights shall end

between his tribes, there is a royal ban

on offers to the idols made by hand.

No more their victims in their clothes of shag

shall fall, although for their own lives they beg.

This is the time of Salomon's revenge!

He's sending out the beasts, the hungry lion,

and fiery dragons with their evil stench,

they're stronger than the stones and fight for Zion.

The wildest men jump back and flee in fear,

yet they are caught, their end is surely near.

Although in anger, still the king is waiting

a moment, for no innocent shall die!

His wrath is heightened and is never bating,

until the idols' bloody priests shall cry.

You hear them call for mercy, wince and shiver,

caught by the lion, no arrows in the quiver.

Who offered humans to the gods of clay

must first in battle fall, be torn apart.

Their village smells like fire and decay,

while dragons breathing smoke burn every heart.

Neither the old nor children are still there,

they are in safety, and in royal care.

Yet there are men, just like the wildest creatures,

still hiding in their huts and facing doom.

They still survive, they show their foremost features:

madness and hatred. Yet mighty lions loom.

The beasts, when full, each single man is gorged,

leave every village, where those gods were forged.

And still there are a few who could escape,

who're heading for the river, but the flood

revenges every single crime and rape

and lets those drown, who once were drinking blood.

No sound to hear, no lion roaring loudly.

The sun goes down. And then a maid speaks proudly:

"A viper tried to reach the eagle's nest

and in the end, it swallowed all his offspring.

The eagle came and saw the scary rest

of all his young, and so he's taken off, king!

He found the viper's brood within a dead cow

devoured it at once. I watched his head bow!

He sat observing, and he saw the beast

just looking for its brood, which was no more.

At first the eagle's nest was just a feast

for vipers - where are all the young it bore?

The eagle watched, in wrath, its shivering tail:

Whoever tries to do no good must fail!"

At last the king, still nodding, gave the order:

"All of you shall obey the Lord's ten laws,

the Jews and even nations across the border

who keep them shall escape the lion's claws.

All subjects shall have figs and wine we've gained!

This land in peace and honor shall be reigned!"

ONCE THERE WAS EDEN

In Eden, the garden, I saw an angel stand

next to the entrance, with a flaming sword:

"Do not touch any apple with your hand",

he whispered, "for their owner is the Lord!"

Then I was still in God's own land unspoiled,

I saw the Cherub's face with glowing eyes;

and on the laden branch a snake, uncoiled,

hissed loudly: "Now you are in paradise!

Your face is happy and your body warm,

you feel the sunshine, and you kiss the rain.

And in the evening there's a cooling storm

which lets you rest and go to sleep again.

But look, the fruit of this old apple tree

is soft like honey, it belongs to thee!"

And Adam lay asleep next to the tree,

his beauty touched my soul, I watched him breathe,

when this old snake again requested me

to pick the apple; I just stood beneath

the mighty tree which would expand my mind

and show me good and bad and let me judge.

The snake was not of any lovely kind,

it hissed again: "Oh Eve, it's time to touch!"

The apple glowed just like the evening sun

in red and gold, my heart was so excited

that I considered, what I could have done,

if I had picked it: Would I be delighted?

My heart was beating fast, when I reached out

and picked the apple; then I heard a shout:

This was the voice of Adam, loud and clear,

which I had heard so many times before:

"Where are you, Eve, when evening's coming near?"

And I addressed the one whom I adore:

"I tasted a fruit, which will delight your mouth

with sweetness, and you will inherit knowledge!"

He took a bite. The wind blew from the South.

We both were safely hidden in a raw ditch.

This very moment taught us both to know

the good things from the evil, right from wrong.

And when the evening sun was sinking low,

we both were singing loud love's sweetest song.

We heard a voice: "Where are the two of you?"

The snake was right. - "We know not what we do."

"I'm naked", Adam whispered full of shame.

"And so am I", I answered from behind

the bush, which covered me. A sword of flame
50

was drawing near. I saw the snake unwind

its twisted tail, and vanish in the meadow.

"Who picked the fruit from the forbidden tree?"

I pointed at the snake. There was a shadow;

the Lord our God spoke angrily to me:

"The snake shall lose its feet and lick the earth,

shall crawl before the woman it seduced.

The woman shall in endless pain give birth,

so she may learn that I am not amused.

"She gave it to me, and I had a bite",

t'was Adam's voice. - "Your life shall be a fight!"

The Cherub drew the sword: "Get out of here!

And don't come back no more!" He closed the door.

The wicked snake cried not a single tear.

I crushed its head. Though there were many more.

Then we were out, were chased from our Lord,

who had bestowed upon us peace and rest.

And in the wilderness a lion roared,

it made us shiver, we had lost our nest.

We begged for mercy, crying day and night,

in endless sorrow, until God appeared:

"I shall protect you with my love and might

from all your foes!" So our God we feared.

Though we could not return to paradise,

we tried to live a life that's fair and wise.

C. M. Herzog, geboren in St. Pölten, Austria; Studium begonnen Spanisch, abgeschlossen Englisch, Französisch an der Universität Wien; Italienisch, Neugriechisch; Studien der Antike: Latein, Altgriechisch; Studien der chinesischen Sprache und Kultur; Arabisch, Hebräisch; ehemals Autor für das Wiener Journal (06/1993-06/94); Beiträge für Literaturzeitschrift etcetera 67/2017, "Nezha und das tosende Meer", etcetera 71/2018, "Meine arabische Quelle aus dem Qur'an"; etcetera 72/2018, "Der Götterschmied" (Lyrik). Ab urbe condita (Autor: Titus Livius, Latein, Ed. C. M. Herzog), Libri XXXIX-XLI, XLII-XLV, XLVI-CXL; Herodoti Historiae (Autor: Herodotus Halicarnasseus, Altgriechisch, Ed. C. M. Herzog); Cornelii Taciti Annalium libri I-VI (Autor: Cornelius Tacitus, Latein, Ed. C. M. Herzog).

C. M. Herzog (German literature):

1. ARIADNE & THESEUS, GEDICHTE

C. M. HERZOG, VERLAG DIE BLAUE EULE, BD. 57

2. DIE VERWANDELTE WELT, LYRIK IN HEXAMETERN

C. M. HERZOG, VERLAG DIE BLAUE EULE, BD. 58

3. HARTMANN DER MÖNCH, BALLADE

C. M. HERZOG, VERLAG DIE BLAUE EULE, BD. 71

4. WEISHEIT UNTER DER SONNE, DRAMA IN FÜNF AKTEN

C. M. HERZOG, VERLAG DIE BLAUE EULE

5. DER ZAUBER DER ANTIKE, GEDICHTE

C. M. HERZOG, VERLAG BOD

ISBN: 9 7837 32 286256

6. DER PRACHTFINK, SATIRISCHE GEDICHTE

C. M. HERZOG, VERLAG BOD

ISBN: 9 7837 39 237350

7. DER STEINEICHE GOLDENE ZWEIGE

C. M. HERZOG, VERLAG BOD

ISBN: 9 7837 44 801263 (Paperback)
ISBN: 9 7837 44 817516 (Hardcover)

8. MEISTER DER STEINERNEN LEUEN

C. M. HERZOG, VERLAG BOD

ISBN: 9 7837 46 098142 (Paperback)
ISBN: 9 7837 46 074016 (Hardcover)

9. APHRODITE LIEBT URANOS

C. M. HERZOG, VERLAG BOD

ISBN: 9 783750 427891 (Paperback)

10. Once there was Eden (English sonnets)

C. M. Herzog, Verlag BoD

ISBN: 9 783752 673173 (Paperback)

C. M. Herzog (philosophy in German):
11. Das Feuer der Weisen

Philosophische Weltbetrachtung aus dem Reichtum der Antike

C. M. Herzog, H. C. Aurelius

Verlag Die blaue Eule, Bd. 61

12. Der Tempel der Seelenruhe

Weisheiten der Antike aus Ost und West

C. M. Herzog, Al-Malik Salomon

Verlag Die Blaue Eule, Bd. 63

Titus Livius (Ab urbe condita):
13. Ab urbe condita

Lib. XLVI-CXL epitomae et fragmenta

Ed. C. M. Herzog, Verlag BoD

ISBN: 9 783748 142065 (Paperback)

14. AB URBE CONDITA

Libri XXXIX-XLI

ED. C. M. HERZOG, VERLAG BOD

ISBN: 9 783749 430338 (Paperback)

15. AB URBE CONDITA

Libri XLII-XLV

ED. C. M. HERZOG, VERLAG BOD

ISBN: 9 783749 448852 (Paperback)

Cornelius Tacitus (Opera):
16. CORNELII TACITI ANNALIUM

Libri I-VI

ED. C. M. HERZOG, VERLAG BOD

ISBN: 9 783752 899139 (Paperback)

Herodotus Halicarnasseus (Historiae):
17. HERODOTI HISTORIAE

Liber I

ED. C. M. HERZOG, VERLAG BOD

ISBN: 9 783746 074290 (Paperback)